MAYA CIVILIZATION

A Complete Overview of The Maya History & Maya Mythology

Eric Brown

© Copyright 2018 by Eric Brown

All rights reserved.

The following eBook is reproduced below with the goal of providing information that is as accurate and reliable as possible. Regardless, purchasing this eBook can be seen as consent to the fact that both the publisher and the author of this book are in no way experts on the topics discussed within and that any recommendations or suggestions that are made herein are for entertainment purposes only. Professionals should be consulted as needed prior to undertaking any of the action endorsed herein.

This declaration is deemed fair and valid by both the American Bar Association and the Committee of Publishers Association and is legally binding throughout the United States.

Furthermore, the transmission, duplication or reproduction of any of the following work including specific information will be considered an illegal act irrespective of if it is done electronically or in print. This extends to creating a secondary or tertiary copy of the work or a recorded copy and is only allowed with an expressed written consent from the Publisher. All additional rights reserved.

The information in the following pages is broadly considered to be truthful and accurate account of facts, and as such any inattention, use or misuse of the information in question by the reader will render any resulting actions solely under their purview. There are no scenarios in which the publisher or the original author of this work can be in any fashion deemed liable for any hardship or damages that may befall them after undertaking information described herein.

Additionally, the information in the following pages is intended only for informational purposes and should thus be thought of as universal. As befitting its nature, it is presented without assurance regarding its prolonged validity or interim quality. Trademarks that are mentioned are done without written consent and can in no way be considered an endorsement from the trademark holder.

Table of Contents

Introduction 5
Chapter 1: The Maya People 6
Chapter 2: The Pre-Classic Period 2000 BCE–250 CE 10
Chapter 3: The Classic Period 250 BCE–900 CE 12
Chapter 4: The Post-Classic Period 950–1539 CE 15
Chapter 5: The Spanish Conquest 1511–1697 CE 18
Chapter 6: The Caste War of Yucatán 1847–1901 CE 21
Chapter 7: Maya Mathematics & Calendar 25
Chapter 8: Maya Religion 30
Chapter 9: Human Sacrifice 36
Chapter 10: Maya Architecture 40
Chapter 11: Maya Culture 45
Chapter 12: Maya Technology 52
Chapter 13: Maya People Today 55
Conclusion 57

Introduction

Congratulations on downloading *Maya Civilization*, and thank you for doing so.

The following chapters will discuss what we famously refer to as the Maya Civilization—its history and the identity of its people. This civilization was believed to have sprouted around 1800 BCE during the Pre-Classic Period in what is now modern-day Belize. This book will cover their evolution from being a collection of small tribes into becoming an empire that sprawled across Mesoamerica and built flourishing city-states. In the Classic Period, the Maya reached their peak in terms of their artistic and mathematical development, their knowledge of astronomy, as well as the evolution of their calendar. They built huge pyramids that served as their temples, and those structures still stand today as historical sites.

Along with the history of their evolution, this book will also dive into the culture and religion of the Maya, with emphasis on their traditions, architecture, and technology. The Maya are especially famous for their tradition of human sacrifice, and this book will share information on that particular ritual, as well as on the reasons why the Maya became known for it. This book delves into many aspects of their culture to illustrate how they lived and grew as a civilization despite the frequent wars between the city-states. Lastly, this book also looks into the descendants of the Maya who are now mostly residing in Yucatán, Mexico and how they strive and fight to keep their traditions alive.

There are plenty of books on this subject on the market, so thanks again for choosing this one! Every effort was made to ensure it is full of as much useful information as possible. Please enjoy!

Chapter 1:
The Maya People

The Maya were the indigenous people of Mexico and Central America, and they once inhabited lands composed of modern-day Mexico, as well as Guatemala, El Salvador, Honduras, and Belize to its south. This indicates that the Maya people had clustered in the central region of the South American continent, most likely to ensure they would be safe from the invasion of other Mesoamerican peoples.

Within that central region, the Maya are believed to have lived in three separate areas with unique characteristics: the northern Maya in the Yucatán Peninsula; the southern lands in northern Guatemala and in Mexico, Belize, and west Honduras; and in the mountainous terrain of southern Guatemala. The Maya of the lowland region is thought to have been the one to build the great stone cities we've come to associate with the entire civilization.

The term "Maya" for the civilization comes from the city of Mayapan, which was the last capital city of the Kingdom during the Post-Classic Period. These same regions today are still home to thousands of archaeological sites of the Maya Kingdom, many of which are still not fully explored. The most important cities include Chichen Itza, Coba, Copan Kalakmul, Tikal, and Uxmal. Surveys and excavations have been conducted by historians to learn more about this ancient people, and tourists are permitted to visit some of the sites.

People who trace their origin to the Maya refer to themselves by the terms Yucatec in the north and Quiche in the south. These are descendants of the civilizations that lived on the same lands of Mesoamerica as their Maya ancestors. These descendants practice a somewhat modified version of the thousand-year-old rituals. They consider themselves linked to their ancestors through their similar languages and traditions and through their ethnic bonds. There are as many as 70 versions of the Maya language in the area, with most descendants also fluent in modern-day Spanish. Languages such as K'iche', Mam, and Q'anjob'al, which are common mainly in the regions of Guatemala, all have Mayan roots.

The Maya people were mostly farmers, with corn or *maize* being their staple crop. They also grew beans, squash, sweet potato, chili peppers, cocoa beans, vanilla beans, and tomatoes, as well as a variety of fruits. They used a farming technique called *milpa*, or what we call today as "slash-and-burn" farming. They would clear the land by cutting down all the trees and bushes and burning the foliage in the spring before the rainy season. Then they would plant their crops. This technique meant that the crop would only be fertile for a few years, so they also had to practice crop rotation every few seasons to ensure a healthy harvest. Besides farming, the Maya were also artisans, with extreme devotion to ceramics, painting, weaving, and textile work.

The Maya were said to have been "discovered" in the 1840s by English explorers John Lloyd Stephens and Frederick Catherwood. They were not the first explorers to visit the civilization of the Maya, but they were the first to document what they found through drawings, maps, and detailed stories. Stephens wrote his observations in *Incidents of Travel in Central America, Chiapas and Yucatán* (1841) and *Incidents of Travel in Yucatán* (1843), accompanied by Catherwood's illustrations.

Only a few Maya texts are believed to have survived the Spanish conquest as the Spaniards had routinely destroyed Maya documents and artifacts. A famous text of the culture, written in the K'iche' language, provides an account of the mythology and history of the people. It begins with their creationism myth, which starts with the following: "This is the account of how all was in suspense, all calm, in silence; all motionless, quiet, and empty was the expanse of the sky."

The culture is said to have been known for its writers and storytellers, but the Maya have also accomplished mathematicians. They used a number system that even included the symbol for zero and allowed for longer calculations to be done more precisely. Their insight into astronomy was more advanced for its time than any other civilization as their astronomers constantly studied the movements of the sun, moon, and visible planets. They were very close in their calculations of the length of the solar year and the lunar cycle, only being off by 0.000198 and over by .0001, respectively.

Unfortunately, with the invasion of the Spaniards, alien diseases such as smallpox and typhoid infiltrated the native population and are thought to have reduced its number by as much as 90% around 1500 to 1600 CE. The spread of Catholicism and the Spanish language also overshadowed the Maya culture and forced its people to assimilate to a changing environment of colonization. The majority of their ancient documents were destroyed by the Spaniards, but a few bark books remain. Their history was also etched in stone, pottery, and cave drawings, giving modern archaeologists valuable insight into this civilization.

The causes for the Maya's fall are numerous, with archaeologists believing everything from political strife, economic instability, infighting between city-states, and environmental causes to be involved in their demise. One of the most central causes is that their cultivated land was not able to meet their food demands. Due to the slash-and-burn farming method, the land would only be viable for a few years at a time before they would be forced to move to another plot to grow their harvest. At its peak, there are believed to have been a population of almost 15 million people occupying the Maya cities. With an increase in population combined with the inability to provide food, it is only natural that economic and social unrest would occur, leading to battles between warring clans and city-states.

Chapter 2:
The Pre-Classic Period 2000 BCE– 250 CE

The Maya are thought to have developed their first civilization in the Pre-Classic Period. Their unearthed settlements in what is now the region of Belize carbon-date to as far back as 2600 BCE. Scientists believe that the first villages were established around 1800 BCE in the Pacific coastline area of the Soconusco region. These people displayed classic early characteristics of the hunter-gatherers of the time as they occupied the rainforests and hills of that region.

The Maya eventually began making their livelihood as farmers. The evidence of corn in the area dates to before 2000 BCE, and surveys of the sediment show manipulation of the terrain. This could be from the burnings of the grass and the cultivation of the harvest. The cultural characteristics of the Maya people are thought to have emerged around 1800 BCE on the Guatemalan coast. The first signs of this were the temples built for various gods. Ceramics and household items have been excavated from ancient villages, and these dates as far back as 2000–1500 BCE. By 1000 BCE, the Maya had spread throughout southern Mexico, Belize, Honduras, and Guatemala.

It was during the Pre-Classic Period that the Maya are thought to have prospered in small villages and basic homes, their society sustained through agriculture. Maize, beans, squash, cacao, and other root crops were their major harvests, and the domestication of animals such as dogs and turkeys were also common. Most tribes depended heavily on their natural habitat and hunted or fished for meat. This sort of lifestyle of foraging for food and hunting as a tribe required a family-centered system to assist in one another's survival. It was also during this period that the culturally impacting Maya pottery and clay figurines began to emerge.

The cities of Palenque, Tikal, and Copan are believed to have been established in this era. The Maya had moved from the coast into the inland areas, though their communities had still been small. There was very little in terms of architectural advancement, only building homes and a temple at each settlement. By the Late Pre-Classic Period, a city known as El Mirador grew to almost 16 square kilometers. Cities began to trade with one another, and the exchange encouraged the propagation of crafts and the arts to influence the culture as a whole. Cities became more expansive, and a council of elders had usually been formed to ensure better management of a growing population in terms of city planning and harvesting decisions. Archaeologists believe that this is when the establishment of Maya kingship began, wherein the people install a ruler in a position of power and that ruler would be held responsible for all decisions made for the entire tribe. The presence of a royal dynasty would continue for the Maya until the Post-Classic Period.

In the coastal plains, Takalik Abaj and Chocoa grew to be two important cities. Meanwhile, Kaminaljuyu emerged in the highlands. What is now northern Belize appears to have been the primary location of the growing Maya Civilization in this era. During the Late Pre-Classic Period, the Maya were already beginning to build in their individual city-states. Tikal and other interior city centers were beginning public construction of plazas and markets, employing the local communities to assist one another with the projects. Archaeologists believe that major building projects involving Maya temples began in this period.

Chapter 3:
The Classic Period 250 BCE–900 CE

The Classic Period of the civilization is believed to have begun when carvings on stelae (statues of the leaders and rulers of the society) began to have dates from the Maya long-count calendar. Research shows the earliest date to have been 292 CE. This period marks the beginning of large construction projects, as well as a trend toward urbanism and artistic and intellectual progress. The Maya continued developing their arts and improving their fields of astronomy and mathematics. Multiple city-states emerged in the region to form alliances and enmities. The largest cities are thought to have populations from 50,000 to 120,000. The cities were connected by roads and a network of travel to ensure an open-trade route.

During the Early Classic Period, the city of Teotihuacán near Mexico City is believed to have intervened at Tikal and other cities to install a Teotihuacán-backed dynasty in 378 CE. The king of Tikal, Chak Tok Ich'aak I, is believed to have died the same day signaling a hostile takeover. The Teotihuacán army that led the invasion installed a new king, Yax Nuun Ahiin, and this resulted in a period where Tikal reigned over the most powerful city in the area by virtue of its alliance with Teotihuacán. This is evidenced by the pottery and architecture created in this era, which bore a resemblance to the Teotihuacán style.

The city of Tikal created an ally out of the city of Calakmul. This alliance was helpful, allowing lesser cities to join in the network and gain the benefit of protection and trade routes. It is common throughout the Classic Period that these cities would gain victory over a rival and then dip into a period of instability. Historians believe that as many as 80 Maya city-states may have existed side by side, in waves of peace and warfare. Tikal and Calakmul are believed to have engaged in warfare many times throughout the Classic Period, as rivalries between city-states often continued for generations after the rulers had died. Depending on the state of tensions between a certain city-state, the state could experience periods of economic growth or decline as well as see a dip in population after the loss of lives in battle.

In the south, Copán was the most influential city, founded in 426 CE by K'inich Yax K'uk' Mo'. This king had ties with Teotihuacán, and he used those ties to influence the city-state. Copán reached the height of development from 695 to 738 CE under the rule of Uaxaclajuun Ub'aah K'awiil. His reign ended when he was taken captive by a rival king of Quiriguá. He was taken to the victory city and decapitated in public. Historians believe the coup may have occurred at the urging of Calakmul to weaken the ally of Tikal. Alliances and rivalries like these between the rulers of city-states were common.

Like many cities from that area of Central America, the city of Teotihuacán is believed to have been abandoned around 900 CE, and the true cause remains unknown. During this period, cities in the northern region of the Yucatán Peninsula continued to be strong, thriving cities despite the mysterious fall of the southern ones. The region may have suffered a political collapse, ending current dynasties and causing unrest. Classic Maya cities used to be based solely on the authority of a single ruler who held all authority. This model was very rigid because it called for the ruler to make decisions regarding wars, harvests, and traditional rituals. Around this era, the individual rule was replaced by a council that did consist of individuals with noble lineage, but they also allowed priests, mathematicians, and other experts in their fields to provide counsel.

Archaeologists believe there was a swift and sudden migration from the south to the north due to the collapse of the powerful city-states. There could have also been environmental factors such as drought and soil degradation that were directly caused by overpopulation and increased food demands. Capital cities and other secondary cities are believed to have been abandoned within a period of 50 to 100 years. Cities stopped creating monuments that were once used to mark the passing of time. The last long-count date is believed to have been inscribed in 909 CE in the city of Toniná. Stelae were no longer raised, and the royal palaces of the rulers were abandoned. Mesoamerican trade routes of the era even shifted to bypass the previously bustling cities, indicating they were uninhabited by then.

Chapter 4: The Post-Classic Period 950–1539 CE

Although major cities collapsed and the causes of the exodus are unclear, there did remain a Maya presence in regions that still had natural water resources. But unlike previous eras wherein abandoned lands were quickly resettled, this was not the case for this era. Instead, activity shifted to the north. The city of Chichen Itza dominated the earlier years of the Post-Classic Period from about 900 to 1250 CE, but after its decline in the 11th century, the region lacked a capital city until the city of Mayapan rose in the 12th century. This is the great city which is believed to have given the Maya its collective name. New cities formed near the capital and new trade networks began to connect neighboring regions. There are reasons to believe that new cities formed along the Gulf and the Caribbean coast to accommodate a trade network involving maritime goods.

The focus changed from a deeply religious nation in the Classic Period to a society focused on economic growth. Instead of relying on priests and the divine rule of kings, the Maya gave more praise to Chac, the Mayan rain god, to provide rain for their crops so they would flourish in their new home. Carvings of this god are found in the buildings of the Post-Classic Period cities such as Uxmal. This type of culture continued until the Spanish arrived in the 16th century.

The Maya Civilization came under the influence of the Toltecs, the name of the people who moved into Mexico after the fall of the city of Teotihuacán. There are significant evidence pointing to this, such as the Maya sculptures and architecture mirroring the Toltec style, as well as the Maya sacrifices to the Toltec rain god, Tlaloc, along with their rain god, Chac. Scholars have yet to pinpoint the political or economic relationship between the two olden cities, but it was clear the Toltecs did influence the Maya during this era.

There were many changes in the Post-Classic Period from the Classic Period. Kaminaljuyu, a city in what is now the region of Guatemala, was abandoned after nearly 2000 years of constant habitation. Cities moved farther inland into more mountainous regions with natural ravine and cavernous terrain. This could have been done so that they could use the natural terrain as protection if neighboring cities decided to wage an attack. With the lack of resources and people, the cities had no choice but to depend on the landscape for protection instead of on large armies, the way they used to.

The Maya of the Yucatán Peninsula had more challenges as they struggled to adjust to the dry climate of the area. They had to switch from using aboveground water sources and adjust to groundwater basins and sinkholes. Cenote Sagrado remains a sacred well in that area for having helped the Maya survive in their new settlement.

The major cities of the Post-Classic era include Chichen Itza and Mayapan. Other cities in the modern-day region of Belize include Santa Rita and Coba, as well Tayasal and Zacpeten in modern-day Guatemala. Mayapan, the capital city, is believed to have been abandoned due to political turbulence sometime in 1448 CE. The Maya states were often governed by a joint rule of a council of elders, but it seems that during this era, the council could appoint a supreme ruler and this may have caused division. This political turmoil along with environmental factors of drought and famine could have accounted for the abandonment of these cities along the Yucatán Peninsula even before the Spanish made contact in 1511.

The area of Guatemala was dominated by several reigning city-states, and the K'iche' had an empire in the Pacific coastal plain. In some regions without a flourishing capital city, the first Spanish explorers had reported thriving markets and lush coastal cities. Trade around the Yucatán cities was still occurring during the later years of the Post-Classic Period and even after the Spanish had arrived. The independent provinces that shared a common culture still managed to work together and maintained a network of good relations to ensure a surviving economy.

But with the ever-growing population and the continuing difficulty in meeting food demands, it is natural for archaeologists to believe that the Maya could not keep up with their provisional requirements. Recent studies have found evidence of environmental factors such as severe droughts, deforestation, and a decline in the population of game animals that would have all combined to create famine. Even the Maya remains dated to this era show severe signs of malnutrition. Though it is believed there was a brief renaissance and rebuilding before the Spanish arrived, it is assumed that the environmental condition did not improve, causing social anxiety and insecure living conditions among the city-states.

The Spanish began their conquest of the Maya in 1524 CE, but it would take them nearly 150 years to achieve complete victory. The main reason was that there was no central Mayan government, only individual city-states that needed to be subjugated separately. Another reason was that the Spanish arrived with dreams of finding gold, but the region did not possess vast quantities of precious metals, and the colonizers became disheartened many times throughout the fight.

Chapter 5:
The Spanish Conquest 1511–1697 CE

Before the year 1524 CE, which is commonly known as the fall of the Maya Empire, the Maya Civilization had had many encounters with explorers. The first recorded interaction between the Maya and the Europeans occurred on July 30, 1502, when Christopher Columbus arrived at Guanaja, Honduras. It was his fourth voyage to the Mesoamerican part of the world.

The account goes that Columbus had sent his brother Bartholomew to explore the nearby land. A large canoe approached, and Bartholomew Columbus boarded and found it to be a Maya trading vessel from Yucatán. The Europeans looted the rich cargo and seized the elderly captain to act as an interpreter for them. The rest of the canoe's passengers were allowed to leave. It is likely that this is where the first impressions and news of the strange pirates and bearded white male invaders spread along the area and came to be passed down. Such stories were even written in the Maya books of *Chilam Balam*.

It has also been told that in 1511, a Spanish vessel was shipwrecked along the Caribbean coast. Twelve survivors made it to the Yucatán coast. They were captured by the Maya and killed in rituals of human sacrifice, but two managed to escape and tell the tale of what they lived through. During the time period of 1517 and 1519, three other Spanish crews visited the coastline of Yucatán and battled with the Maya.

The notion that the Maya were driven from their cities by Spanish conquistadors is not entirely correct. Most major cities were already abandoned when the Spaniards first arrived.

Though the K'iche' and the Cachiquel groups in Guatemala were attempting to rebuild, they were foiled when they came under the control of the Aztecs. Additionally, conflicts within the Maya lands had already resulted in divisions between the city-states, causing the empire to fall from its former glory.

The Spanish colonization of the Maya lands officially began in 1521 when Francisco de Montejo petitioned the King of Spain for the right to conquer the Yucatán. In 1524, Hernán Cortés conquered the Aztec Empire and sent his lieutenant, Pedro de Alvarado, to investigate and conquer the nearby Maya city-states in what is now northern Guatemala. It is believed he defeated Tenochtitlan on October 12, 1524, with 300 infantry, 4 cannons, 180 cavalry units, and up to 3000 warriors from Mexico. Before that, he had marched through the Maya province of Acalan where he recruited up to 600 more soldiers. He had a difficult journey southward along the Maya Mountains and lost most of his horses due to the terrain. The group got lost near Lake Izabal and came close to starvation before they captured a Maya who led them to safety. Having found them already weak, Alvarado easily conquered the nearby city-states after preying on the rivalries between the rulers to cause infighting. The introduction of new European diseases also decimated the struggling population, which had no immunity to these foreign illnesses.

The K'iche' capital, Q'umarkaj, fell to Alvarado in 1524. Next came the collapse of Zaculeu and the Itza capital of Nojpeten. During the Battle of Utatlan, the K'iche' Maya was defeated. Unlike the Aztec which had been a centralized community, the Maya had been spread out into city-states, and they resisted Spanish rule with bloody rebellions for nearly a hundred years. Unlike their victories over the Mesoamerican empires in Mexico and Central America, defeating the Maya had not been a swift undertaking, but eventually, the Spaniards won against the last Mayan city in the Peten in 1697.

The Conquistadors had traveled to the Mesoamerican region in hopes of finding gold and silver. Trace amounts were found along Columbia and Ecuador and were transported back to Spain, but these regions were not as rich in metals as the Spanish had been led to believe. They enslaved the Maya and divided up the land between the generals of the army and the government bureaucrats who came from Spain to assist in ruling the new nations.

The Maya were required to convert to Christianity, and those who refused had been arrested and tortured. The Spanish were also active in destroying Mayan artifacts. Much of their culture, writing, and art were destroyed; only a few sacred texts had been saved and passed down to the succeeding generations. Many of the native peoples suffered. Bloody rebellions were common as the Maya were reluctant subjects of this new foreign government. They were repressed forcibly, and loss of life was significant. A man by the name of Bartolomé de Las Casas passionately argued for the rights of the Maya in the Spanish court; his efforts were ultimately thwarted, but they were not without any positive impact.

Some remote Maya villages did survive on their own and continued their day-to-day life. They maintained a traditional diet of tortilla, maize, and beans and kept their traditional crafts of basket-weaving and ceramic-making. It is assumed that their agriculture became easier and more advanced with the help of the steel tools that the Spaniards brought, and trade and education in the local crafts continued well after the conquest. The administration of the colonies would also encourage the traditional economy; there was a demand for local goods. However, the Mayan ceramics and textiles would thereafter take on a more European leaning.

Chapter 6:
The Caste War of Yucatán 1847–1901 CE

A 19th century revolt by the indigenous Maya people of Yucatán, Mexico that lasted for nearly fifty years is known today as the Caste War of Yucatán. The Maya revolted against the European descendants called the Yucatecos, who held the most political and economic control in the region. The inhabitants of the northwest Yucatán region fought with the independent Maya people of the southeast.

During the Spanish colonial times, there existed a caste system wherein those born in Spain with pure Spanish blood stands at the top and the indigenous people of the land lies at the very bottom. The indigenous population was concentrated in the Campeche-Mérida region. In the Yucatán region, the Maya outnumbered the European-descended groups by nearly 3:1, and it was by 5:1 near the east in terms of the population ratio. The elites controlled the Maya, and the Church and the military aligned with the stronger classes.

The success of the Mexican War of Independence inspired the subjugated Maya people in the Yucatán. They organized their own resistance to gain independence from Spain, and they joined with the Mexican government which aimed for centralization of the city-states despite many provinces revolting against the notion. After the war against Texas, the Mexican government imposed a number of high taxes to bear the costs, even imposing a trade tax.

On May 2, 1839, a protest led by Santiago Imán created a rival government in Tizimín. He and his followers took over

Valladolid, Izamal, Espita, and lastly, the city of Mérida on the Yucatán Peninsula. He convinced the Maya population to join the cause and even gave them access to weapons for the first time since the Spanish Conquest. With the support of the Maya, he prevailed in battle and proclaimed Yucatán to be an independent republic as of 1841.

The head of the Mexican government, Antonio López de Santa Anna, refused to accept their independence and imposed a blockade. Invasion followed, and the Yucatán struggled against the authority of the Mexicans and its divided factions. One faction based in Campeche led by Santiago Méndez feared reintegration and a sudden attack on the region by the United States at the northern border. In Mérida, Miguel Barbachano leaned toward reintegration to gain the safety of Mexico. Both leaders convinced many Maya citizens into their armies as soldiers.

The War started in defense of Indian land against private ownership due to the increased production of the agave plant. This was an industrial fiber at the time, harvested to make rope. Once the plant's value was discovered, the wealthy Spanish Yucatecos created huge plantations to cultivate it on a large scale and began to encroach on Maya communal lands. They abused Maya workers and treated them poorly, underpaying them for their hard labor.

Santiago Méndez, who was leading a faction near Campeche, arrested Antonio Ay, the principal Maya leader of Chichimilá, and executed him in the Valladolid town square. Méndez burned down the entire town of Tepich, and several other Maya towns were destroyed, with many people killed in the subsequent months. Cecilio Chi, Maya leader of Tepich, attacked the city of Tepich on July 30, 1847, and decreed that any non-Maya would be killed. By 1848, the Maya forces had taken over the majority of Yucatán except for the walled cities of Campeche and Mérida along the southern coast. In an 1849 letter, Chi wrote that Méndez's goal was to "put every Indian, big and little, to death" but that the Maya had responded in kind. He wrote, "It has pleased God and good fortune that a much greater portion of them [whites] than of the Indians [have died]."

Miguel Barbachano, the Yucatecan governor, prepared to evacuate the city of Mérida but could not send out the order due to a lack of paper in the capital city. Troops managed to invade the city and make significant advances.
The reason for the Maya's defeat is unclear. Historians believe they might have abandoned their posts to tend their fields, or they may not have been able to feed their army any longer and became frustrated with the long war efforts.

By 1850, the Maya occupied two regions and a stalemate had developed among the northwestern tribes. Positioned in the middle was the jungle region. In 1850, an apparition of the "Talking Cross" appeared to inspire the Maya to keep fighting. The apparition was believed to have been God communicating with the Maya. Chan Santa Cruz, translated to mean "Small Holy Cross," became a religious mecca for the resistance and inspired new religious meaning in the soldiers and supporters. The followers of the Cross became known as the "Cruzob" people.

The largest independent Maya state was called Chan Santa Cruz, and its capital city was given the same name. The United Kingdom recognized Chan Santa Cruz as an independent "de facto" nation due to the trade routes between the region and British Honduras. This resulted in a signed international treaty, though it was never formally ratified by either party. The region had extensive trade relations with British Honduras and had a significantly larger militia than the British colony. For these reasons, the British felt it advantageous to maintain good relations.

When the Maya laid siege on the city of Bacalar and killed British citizens, the British Government assigned Sir Spenser St. John to break relations with the indigenous free states, particularly the Maya free state. In 1893, the British Government signed the Spenser Mariscal Treaty that ceded the Maya state's lands to Mexico. Chan Santa Cruz was then occupied by the Mexican army.

The conflict ended in 1915 when the region agreed to recognize the Mexican government. General Francisco May signed a formal treaty with the government of Mexico to represent another step taken toward peace. In September 1915, the Mexican government sent General Salvador Alvarado to restore order in Yucatán. He worked to implement reforms which eliminated conflicts between the regions.

The last skirmish in the area is documented as having occurred in April 1933 when the Mexican army took a force into a remote village that never recognized the establishment of Mexican law. Two Mexican soldiers along with five Maya citizens were killed in the village of Dzula. This is the last historically noted incident that occurred in a conflict that lasted almost 90 years.

Chapter 7:
Maya Mathematics & Calendar

At its cultural peak around 250 to 900 CE, the Maya created a very sophisticated numbering system that was possibly the most advanced in the entire world during the time. The Maya, like many Mesoamerican cultures of the period, used a vigesimal numbering system that was founded on a base of 20 units: 0–19 with zero included as a numeral. This was most likely inspired by the natural use of the fingers and toes to count. The numerals had three symbols: zero represented by a shell shape, five by a bar, and one by a single dot. Adding and subtracting became simpler when they only needed to count dots and bars, and this allowed even the uneducated to do calculations related to trade and commerce easily.

Because of the simplicity of these symbols, it is believed that the Maya used objects from nature itself when practicing their math—i.e., real sticks, stones, and shells had been used to manipulate numbers and work on problems. Scientists have found that all the major mathematical functions (addition, subtraction, division square roots, multiplication) could be performed using this simple base system. The Maya mathematical system is even now being taught in Yucatán, Mexico, where the descendants of the Maya people are most greatly concentrated. It is especially taught to the indigenous children in the area to encourage understanding and appreciation of their culture.

Maya numbers are written from bottom to top instead of horizontally like most of the world does today. For example, the number 12 is presented as two bars and two dots on top. The number 19 is three bars and four dots on top. Numbers greater than 19 were represented the same way, but with a dot placed above the number for each group of 20 it had. This place value format used the powers of 20: 1, 20, 400, 8000, and 160,000. The number 32 would contain all the symbols for the number 12, but with an additional dot to signify the addition of 20. The number 401 would use a dot in the first position, a zero in the second and another dot in the third to first signify 400 (20 × 20) and then the addition of one. It is commonly believed that the society used cocoa beans on the ground to do their calculations.

The names for common numerals are as follows:

0: xix im
1: hun
2: caa
3: ox
4: can
5: hoo
6: uac
7: uuc
8: uaxac
9: bolon
10: lahun
20: hun kal
40: ca kal
60: ox kal
80: can kal
100: hoo kal
200: ka hoo kal
300: ox hoo kal
400: hun bak
800: ca bak
1200: ox bak

1,600: can bak
2,000: hoo bak
8,000: pic
160,000: calab
3,200,000: kinchil
64,000,000: alau

It is believed that the Pre-Classic Maya and their Mesoamerican neighbors formulated the concept of the zero integers around 30 BCE. There is archaeological evidence that shows them working with integers up to the hundreds of millions. It would sometimes take lines of dashes and circles to represent the number. The concept of a zero was unknown in most Classic societies with the exception of the Gupta Empire in India, but zero days and zero years exist in the Maya calendar, and the Maya society understands its value and how it may be used to multiply and add enormous numbers.

The Maya also considered some numbers sacred over other numbers. The number 20, which formed the basis of their counting system, was one of those numbers, most likely because of the ten toes and ten fingers that a human could count on. The number five also had religious significance as this was the number of digits on a foot or a hand. Thirteen was considered to be a number for the original Maya gods. The number 52 was sacred and was established to be the number of years in a "bundle," which is a unit that the Maya used as a concept similar to the concept of "century" we use today. The number 400 was considered to represent the Maya gods of the night.

The Maya also used head glyphs as numerical symbols to represent the gods. The number one was depicted as a young earth goddess, the number two for a god of sacrifice, and so on.

The glyphs are very similar to each other, and this presented archaeologists with some difficulty when decoding them. The number was also sometimes written as compounds. The number 13 would use the glyph for 10 plus the glyph for number three. This combined with the usual shells, bars, and dots that formed the base level of Maya mathematics.

Mathematicians were an important and respected part of Maya society. This is evident in the Maya wall paintings discovered by historians long after the society collapsed. Maya mathematicians and their scribes can be identified as the ones carrying number scrolls in their arms. Most historians agree that the first mathematician identified on a glyph in wall art was a female figure, indicating that the Maya did not prefer male mathematicians over female.

Due to this very precise concept of math, the Maya were more accurate than other societies in their astronomical observations and calculations. Considering that they were working from only naked eye observation, their numbers are very comparable to modern data. They charted the movements of Jupiter, Venus, the moon, Mars, and Mercury. They also tracked the position of the sun along the horizon to gauge when the seasons would change. They were especially captivated by the constellations in the night sky and believed them to be the gods watching over them. The estimated the length of a lunar month to be 29.5308 days. Today's modern value is 29.53059. They calculated the length of a solar year to be 365.242 days, extremely close to today's modern value of 365.242198 and far more accurate than any used in Europe at the time. The length of 365 days means that the calendar only fell out of step with the seasons by one day every four years. Again, this was achieved while working only with naked eye observation. By comparison, the Julian calendar used in Europe during the Roman Empire had an error of one day every 128 years.

It is believed the Maya had two calendars: the Tzolkin and the Haab. The Tzolkin had 260 days which was divided into 13 "months" of 20 days each. These months were named after gods while the 20 days were numbered by using the digits 0 to 19. This was their religious ritual calendar. Every 52 years counted as an interval, and after that time period, the calendar would reset itself and begin from zero. The Haab calendar was a 365 day civil calendar which consisted 18 months and contained dates of religious and agricultural events that the entire society would participate in. The Maya had a great understanding of celestial bodies for the time period and could even predict solar eclipses. They used the astrological cycles to aid in harvesting and planting their crops, and these events would also be labeled on the Haab calendar.

It is important to note that despite the advanced thinking of their time, the Maya and Mesoamerican mathematical numbering systems had no influence on the European and Asian systems due to a significant geographical divide. This works reciprocally—they were also not influenced by the European and Asian systems, and all advancements in their thinking are credited solely to the Maya society. Their mathematics allowed the Maya to have one of the most accurate calendar measurements of all the ancient societies, to construct huge step-pyramids, and to engage in a complex system of trade with neighboring societies.

Chapter 8: Maya Religion

The Maya religion is based on the belief that everything in the world contains *k'uh* (sadness), and this is used to explain the spirituality of all animate and inanimate objects in the universe. The belief is that this establishes sanctity between all life forms—between the earth and humans.

When beginning to look at the Maya creation myth, it is critical to differentiate between the two sources that have been unearthed. These include the books *Popol Vuh* and *Chilam Balam*. *Popol Vuh* is connected to the traditional Maya highland region in what is now the country of Guatemala. It contains the traditional myths, histories, and prophecies that historians associate with the Maya. The anthologies of *Chilam Balam* are associated typically with the Yucatán area of Mexico and were written by a priest whose name translated to *Chilam Balam*. These books are from around 1500 CE after Spanish Conquistadors had already invaded the Maya empire, and historians believe there is Spanish influence on this in the stories of *Chilam Balam*.

Earth is believed to have created by Huracán, the sky and wind god. The earth and sky were connected, and there was no space in between for anything living to flourish. A Ceiba tree was planted. The tree's roots grew into the underworld, and the branches grew up in the atmosphere. The trunk grew big enough to leave room on earth for animals, humans, and plants to roam across the land. Animals and plants were believed to be in existence long before humans, but the Maya believed the gods were unhappy with them because animals could not speak to praise the gods. Because of this sole reason, the gods created humans to praise them.

There are three creation stories detailed in the *Popol Vuh* of the highland Maya: people made from mud, people made from wood, and people made from maize. The first creation tale told that people were made from mud, but they were not the most productive and were not very rational or capable of high-thinking. According to ancient texts, the men and women "spoke but had no mind." They were not even technically mortal. The gods were displeased with them and destroyed them with water.

Next, the gods created women from reeds and men from wood. These creations could pass as human beings, but they possessed no souls and they did not properly honor the gods. They were also immortal and supposedly died for only three days before rising from the dead. (This very closely follows the stories of Christianity.) This society was destroyed by being boiled in hot water. The Maya believed that those who survived their destruction became the monkeys that roamed their jungles.

The third creation was that of the modern-day Maya humans. The Maya believe they are created from maize dough and possessed the blood of the gods. The first batch created consisted of four men and four men. They were believed to be too wise by the gods and were destroyed by them as well, fearing that they'll become threats. But the Heart of the Heaven, or Huracán the sky god, clouded their eyes and minds so they would become less wise and less of a threat to their superiors. In this story, Huracán is known as the Heart of Earth, Heart of Heaven, and Heart of Sky for his mercy to this creation.

Despite the different creation myths, the most important note historians made was the notion of destruction common among these societies. New humans were created then destroyed to make room for another civilization. This is not synonymous with the Maya notion of "the end of the world" but simply recognizes that they believe in the notion of the end of humanity and in a new civilization created by the mercy of their gods. The gods destroyed these civilizations because they would not worship them, and they would not have unworthy subjects who could not praise them.

Though there are Maya deities, the most significant gods often morphed with the less notable ones and shared characteristics of both gods at the same time. Some could even have conflicting traits. These diverse and fluid personalities that shift many times make it difficult for historians to identify and isolate each Maya deities. This is true for their appearance as well.

Huracán is a significant god as shown in the creation myth. He is also known as the "giver of life" in prayer in the *Popol Vuh* book. This prayer suggests he was important as a creator. He is associated with the Quiche Maya of Guatemala and supposedly created the earth and took mercy on the maize people who are the current human civilization. He is the lord of the fire, storms, and wind.

Itzam Ná and Ix Chebel Yax are two gods associated with creation as well. Itzam Ná is drawn as a long-nosed old man, or sometimes as an iguana. His wife is Ix Chebel Yax who is very high in the hierarchy of the gods. K'inich Ajaw is sometimes known as God G or Kinich Ahau, the "Sun-faced Lord." He is portrayed as being born in the East and aging and setting in the West just as the sun does. He was a war advisor to the underworld and could also transform into a jaguar. Sun deities are to be feared and worshipped at the same time; though they give the life-giving properties of the sun, they can also send too many rays to create drought and ruin the harvest. Chac was the counterpart god to K'inich Ajaw, known as God B. He is believed to be both human and reptile and is often depicted with a serpent, lightning bolt, or an axe. This god is sometimes depicted as being blue with whiskers. The Maya believed he also had the power to create thunder, lightning, and clouds. He was also to be feared and worshipped because he brought rains for the people and crops but also created floods. He demanded blood sacrifices for payment for the rains.

The maize god, Hun H'unahpu, was also considered an important celestial being and was referred to as God E. He was believed to have created the modern humans that lived in the lowland Yucatec Maya using his own maize and blood. He was seen as a symbol of fertility and was depicted as a handsome young man with long black hair.

God K, or K'awil, is the god responsible for protecting the royal bloodline and was also linked to lightning. He is depicted with piercings of a torch and carrying a blade and has a snout on one foot and a snake on the other. He is believed to have discovered maize and cocoa when he struck his lightning bolt on a mountain.

Ix Chel, or God O, is the goddess of the rainbows. Rainbows symbolize harmony and peace in Western culture, but this is not the case for the Maya. They believed that rainbows were the "flatulence of demons" and that they brought sickness. When her form was believed to bring bad luck, she was drawn as clawed and fanged for this reason. But due to the often duplicitous traits of the gods the Maya attached to their deities,

Ix Chel could also represent childbirth and fertility. When pictured in those contexts, she is depicted as very beautiful and youthful.

A popular legend in Maya religious culture is that of the Hero Twins, two brothers named Xbalanque and Hunahpu who survived adventures in the underworld. Their stories are chronicled in the *Popol Vuh*. The Twins' father was the god Hun H'unahpu—he and his brother were lured to the underworld to be decapitated. But because he was immortal, his head survived and gave fruit. His head then fell onto the goddess Xquic who gave birth to the Hero Twins.

These twins faced many challenges in their heroic story to return home, but the most significant was their journey through Xibalba, the Maya underworld. They were summoned there after they played a noisy ballgame that disturbed the underworld lords. The lords challenged the twins, but the brothers were cunning and wise, getting the best of the lords. Hunahpu and Xbalanque grew bored with the challenges and thought of a way to escape by disguising themselves. They performed a trick for the lords wherein they sacrificed a person and brought the person back to life. The lords were impressed and asked them to perform the trick on them. But Xbalanque and Hunahpu were smart and seized the opportunity. Instead of bringing the lords back to life, the twins left them dead and declared the underworld as a place for sinners to be held captive. The Hero Twins and the lords of Xibalba are believed to be night stars. The Maya believe that their kings would have to follow the trials of Xbalanque and Hunahpu in the underworld after their death in order to make it to heaven.

Regarding hell and heaven, the Maya believed in various levels and called them the underworld, middle, and upper world. The upper world consists of thirteen levels while the middle world was only one level. The underworld contained nine different levels of hell. The Ceiba tree is believed to grow through all the levels and provided the five cardinal directions they believed in—the four directions and the center. The most important direction to the Maya was the east where the sun rises. They associated it with rebirth because they believed the sun is born daily.

Chapter 9:
Human Sacrifice

Despite the common tales of Maya human sacrifice, not all religious rituals required it. Sacrifices were most commonly performed in a mix of religious ceremonies because blood was seen as the nourishment for the deities. Sacrifices were also given during important ceremonies such as dedicating a new building or celebrating the enthronement of a new ruler. Human sacrifice is evident in Maya culture from at least the Classic Period (250–900 CE) right until the final stages of the Spanish conquest. These events are written in the Maya hieroglyphic texts of the era and are also depicted in Maya art. Even archaeological analysis of skeletal remains shows evidence of human sacrifice.

Several methods were used by the Maya to perform their rituals of human sacrifice, including decapitation, heart removal, and arrow sacrifice. The method depended on which type of ceremony was occurring. The sacrifice of an enemy king was considered the most important ritual. It required some sort of playacting, a reenactment of the capture of the ruler in front of a crowd—the decapitation of the Maya maize god by the death gods.

In 738 CE, the king K'ak' Tiliw Chan Yopaat of Quiriguá captured his overlord, Uaxaclajuun Ub'aah K'awiil and then decapitated him. Historians believe that these events are illustrated in the Maya texts by the symbol of an axe. Sacrifice by decapitation is also depicted in Maya art. They may have taken place after the victim was beaten, burnt, or disemboweled. Decapitation sacrifices are also shown on ancient reliefs at Chichen Itza in two of the ballcourts.

Ballcourt sacrifices were common to reenact the story where the Hero Twins decapitated their ballgame opponents.

In the Post-Classic Period, the common form of sacrifice was heart extraction. This was influenced by their neighbors, the Aztec Empire. These most commonly occurred at the steps of the pyramid or in the temple's courtyard. The sacrificial victim was stripped naked, painted blue, and forced to wear an elaborate headdress. Four attendants, also painted blue and representing the four cardinal directions, stretched the sacrifice out over a large stone. This would push the victim's chest out. An official called the *nacom* used a knife to saw into the ribs and cut out the beating heart. The knife was most commonly made of flint stone. The *nacom* would pass the heart to the priest, or *chilan*, who smeared the blood upon the temple to complete the sacrifice.

For some rituals, the helpers may have even thrown the victim down the stone steps where they would be skinned, except sometimes their heads and feet would be kept. The *chilan* would dress in the victim's skin and perform a dance to symbolize the rebirth of life. If it was not a courageous warrior who became a sacrificial victim, then the corpse could even be cut into pieces and eaten by other attendants and bystanders. If it was a warrior, the hands and feet would be given to the *chilan* who, if they were also a soldier, kept the bones as a trophy.

Arrow sacrifice involved being killed with bows and arrows. This type of sacrifice is recorded as early as the Classic Period on the walls of the Tikal Temple in graffiti art. The victim was stripped of clothing and painted blue. They would be tied to a stake while a ritualistic dance was performed around them. Genital blood would be drawn and smeared along the temple.

The victim's heart would be marked with a white mark to present it clearly as a target to the archers during the arrow ceremony. The dancers performed their traditional dance in front of the victim and would shoot arrows until the chest was filled with them.

The most common sacrifice was bloodletting, which is the spilling of blood in human sacrifice. The Maya practice of bloodletting was mostly done by the royal line. The Maya believed the gods had spilled their blood to create humanity, so they now demanded human blood in return. Along with human blood, the Maya would also offer to the god's other precious items such as masks, human bone, shells, gold, and ceremonial tools.

Bloodletting was common during significant dates on the Maya calendar such as births, new kings rising to the throne, and anniversaries. Royals who participated in the practice spent many days before the ritual preparing themselves through purification. Both women and men from the royal family were to perform these rituals, and they made sacred tools to use on themselves. The tools were most commonly made of stingray spines and had glyphs carved into them to show religious significance. Blood was let from various parts of the body, and it was often a contest to see which area could provide the most significant amount of blood. Another form of overlooked communication with the gods was lowering children into wells in the belief that they could speak to the gods. After hours in the well, the children would be pulled back up so they could relay the message of the gods.

It is important to note that there were many skirmishes with the Spanish regarding human sacrifice. The Spanish ship, Santa María de la Barca, set sail along the coast of Central

America in 1511. After thirteen days, half the survivors made it to the Yucatán coast where they were seized by a Mayan lord, Halach Uinik. The captain of the ship and four companions were sacrificed, and their flesh was served at a feast. In 1529, another disastrous Spanish assault on Uspantán occurred and the captives were sacrificed to one of the Hero Twins. Such occurrences were common until the 16th century, in which many shipwrecked survivors and Spanish missionaries were sacrificed. This served only to exacerbate the relations between the Spanish and the Maya.

It is important to note that the Maya religion held no concept whatsoever that there was anything wrong with human sacrifice. It was not done out of spite or revenge to the individual. In fact, they simply believed the individuals being sacrificed were moving on and that their sacrifice would greatly please the gods, giving them a higher rank in heaven.

Chapter 10: Maya Architecture

Thanks to their advanced mathematical skill for that time period, the Mayan architects built cities of stone that remain to this day, long after the decline of their civilization. These stone structures were set with hydraulic cement and enabled the Maya structure to survive centuries of abandonment, followed by excavation from scientists to learn about these ancient civilizations. Some remain standing to this day and serve as tourist sites. The Maya decorated these buildings with detailed stone carvings and paint, often depicting the important political or religious occurrences of their city-state as a way of recording their history.

The Maya designed their city-states using what architects call today as a plaza-central plan. They arranged clusters of important buildings around a central open plaza layout. This placed important buildings such as the palaces, temples, and schools in the location of residential areas. Historians have found these were not arranged as orderly as it sounds. Due to the Maya building their city-states on uneven terrain to avoid floods and for their city's protection, these plaza shapes could be very irregular. In the center of the cities, the temples, palaces, and a ball court to play the game of Poc-a-Toc were linked to dense residential areas that grew into sparser villages the further away they are from the city. Stone walkways linked the residential areas.

The Maya kings lived in stone palaces near the city temples, but the commoners lived in small houses away from the center. The homes tended to be bunched close together for anthropological needs. Having extended family living close by provided support when necessary, especially for couples with young children. The houses were made mostly of wood, poles, and thatch. As the wood and leaves of the walls wore away due to natural weathering, they would take it as a sign to rebuild on the same foundation. Because the commoners' ground was further away from the high ground of the city center, most of these homes have been lost due to flooding or the encroaching jungle terrain.

Maya temples were built of limestone with platforms on the top where wooden structures could be erected. They were built with astronomy and the alignment of the sun, moon, or other visible planets in mind. For example, the Lost World Complex at Tikal has a temple pyramid that faces three other temples. When standing at one pyramid you can see the other temples aligned with the rising and setting sun. Temples were built in the shape of pyramids with steep steps built to the top. These provided a platform where religious ceremonies and sacrifices took place and a point where all citizens could gather in the courtyard and watch.

Archaeologists have been able to decipher Maya historical events and the detail behind their religious ceremonies due to the artwork and glyphs carved into the stones of the temple. The famous Hieroglyphic Stairway at a temple in Copán is an example of detailed stone carvings that remain to this day. Because there are so few remaining artifacts from the Maya era, these carvings give an important insight for historians to piece together the history of the Maya. The pyramids also acted as tombs for the Maya rulers and their families, sacrifice victims, as well as precious goods that were needed to be kept with the royal family. Because of the necessity for more space, archaeologists have found that the outside pyramid structures sometimes reveal complete but diminishing pyramids inside

A notable example of a typical Maya temple structure would be the Palenque's Temple of Inscriptions believed to be built around 700 CE. A single staircase climbs several levels to the top to a platform that has several chambers, believed to be for the priests. The pyramid has nine levels that are said to represent the nine levels of the Maya underworld, Xibalba. There is a secret passageway that descends to the tomb of King Pakal in the center. The passageway has thirteen steps to represent the thirteen Maya heavens.

Another unique example of Maya architecture is the Pyramid of the Magician at Uxmal which is believed to have been built around 600 CE. It is distinctive because of the rounded corners that make it seem almost oval in shape. It is the only one of its kind that has been found in the standing structures left by the Maya Civilization.

The royal palaces were built from the same materials as the other homes and in the same manner—limestone with rubber, wooden structures on top, and a thatch roof. Some roofs would have corbelled roofing where flat stones would be piled upon one another in overlapping patterns for protection. This type of roofing is found more commonly in structures dating the Post-Classic Period, indicating that the Maya must have found this more successful and implemented it in later structures over the earlier thatch roof.

The palaces were built as spacious, open buildings with courtyards and other smaller structures that acted as homes to servants, outdoor eating areas, or watch towers for guards. There were plenty of rooms to act as cooking areas, sleeping quarters, classrooms for children, and luxury rooms that double as steam rooms and bathrooms. Some palaces were significantly larger than others, leading historians to believe they also acted as offices where councilmen met to discuss wars, trade, and agriculture. These palaces were the place where royalty and noblemen met with commoners and hosted visiting royalty from other city-states. Statewide feasts, ceremonies for the new king, royal dances, and community events took place at the palaces as well.

Historians believe religious ceremonies were also hosted at the royal palaces and not just at the pyramids, based on the evidence of the Nunnery complex at Uxmal. The northern building of that palace has thirteen doorways representing the thirteen levels of heaven that the Maya believe in. The southern building has nine doorways to represent the nine levels of the underworld, and the western building has seven doorways which were considered the mystic number of the earth.

The ceremonial game of Poc-a-Toc was a pastime for the common and nobility alike, but the game also held important religious and spiritual significance, with the losers, or sometimes even the winners, being sacrificed in the belief they would make it to heaven. The game's ball courts were huge rectangular fields with sloped walls. In the later Post-Classic Period, the walls were changed to vertical walls. They were placed distinctly near the center of the city for their importance to the culture. Some cities even had more than one. The most famous one from the Maya is the court found at Copán believed to be built around 800 CE. It is perfectly framed in the view of the hills around the area. Archaeologists believe that since these courts had a religious significance, they were positioned carefully between the north and the south to maintain the balance of the earthly world and the underworld.

Small stone structures that acted as sweat baths were also found, with huge stones where heated water was poured. There were often small adjoining spaces to be used for changing clothes. They are usually found by ball courts and in the royal palace area and were used for both cleaning and religious purposes.

Another unique aspect of Maya architecture is the corbelled arches they built to resemble the classic arch that originated from the ancient Greek. The stones would be aligned in long patterns to make the appearance of an arch in an inverted "V" shape. The blocks were stacked in successive steps from opposite sides and closing in at the center. The arches had severe limitations due to it being structurally unstable. For the arch to be durable, it would have to be tall and narrow and often made the rooms dark and narrow due to a lack of light. These arches became known as the Maya arches and formed the base for all Maya structures.

Chapter 11: Maya Culture

Marriage was an important religious ritual and an event of celebration in Maya culture. Marriages were arranged and the parties come from the same social class. Couples could be matched at a very young age, sometimes even promised to each other as infants. Historians believe that the ages of Maya individuals at the time of marriage were linked to the Maya population as a whole: when the population was low, marriages would occur even if the individuals were young so they could reproduce sooner and repopulate.

Priests preformed the marriage ceremonies most often at the bride's home. They would burn incense to pray for a fruitful marriage. A feast would be cooked to celebrate the joining. The exchanging of gifts were common, either gold or precious items of significance. If the marriage was considered not successful by either party, the couple could divorce. Although there is no ritual for a divorce described in Maya text, historians have found that it was an acceptable option, and the couple could peacefully part ways.

The typical Maya family averaged five to seven members according to modern archaeologists. The family all lived together and followed traditional gender roles: the men farmed and hunted while the women would cook and weave in the home. The girl children helped their mothers while the boys, when old enough, would learn from their fathers and help with physical labor. Children only went to school if they came from a noble family. The role of the extended family was common among the Maya. Often, newlywed couples would live with the groom's parents until they had a child of their own. Then they might leave to establish their own home. Later in life, elderly parents might return to their children's home to be taken care of in their old age.

A typical home for a Maya family would depend on their region. Groups who lived in south Guatemala would live in one-room huts built out of poles and covered with dried mud for protection from the elements. Other groups in the highlands would live in houses with tile roofs, the walls made of boards or poles. Most of the Maya were farmers, so the diet of corn was a staple in most meals; tamales or tortillas was also common. The kernels were boiled, ground down into a paste, then shaped by hand into flat tortillas before being cooked on an open griddle. Other crops they grew included beans, squash, pear, sweet potato, cocoa beans, vanilla beans, tomatoes, as well as a variety of fruits. All these items were rotated in their diet, as well as the occasional turkey or rabbit for meat. After the Spanish came, they introduced domesticated pigs to the Maya who began to develop their traditional recipes with pork.

The Maya were unique in the sense they did not domesticate large animals for their needs like other civilizations in the area did. They raised dogs, turkeys, and ducks for food, but they hunted deer, rabbits, and boar in the wild, as well as fished. They used every part of the animal for food, tools, or clothing and did not waste the animal out of respect. Animal skin was commonly used to make clothing. The clothing would be decorated with paint or embroidery in designs of other humans or of nature. There would be religious significance to these designs. In fact, it is said that the decorative designs for a woman's traditional attire would appear in their dreams. A woman's traditional attire included three pieces: the *huipil*, a long, sleeveless tunic; the *enredo*, a skirt that would wrap around to cover the lower half of the body; and the *quechquémitli*, a shoulder cape. Men also wore traditional tunics but with less decoration.

The society was broken into a class structure with four main classes. By rank, they were the nobility (Almehenob'), priesthood (Ah'kinob'), the commoners (Ah'chembal uinieol'), and the slaves (Pencat'ob'). At the top were nobles, with the King being the most powerful. The King's role was hereditary, so power was passed down to the son after the father's passing. The priests in the society were the next most powerful because they were the advisors to the king and performed the religious ceremonies. Artists, mathematicians, scribes, medicine men, and architects fell into this class. In order to have received education in their field of study, they would have to come from a noble family. The next level of people were the commoners. The majority of Maya society were farmers, so most people fell into this category. The lowest rung of social classes were the slaves who were prisoners captured during wars, or people who had broken the law and was being punished. They would be used for physical labor when it came time to construct roads or pyramids.

Archaeologists believe they have even found insight into the Maya standards of beauty, and it is quite unique. They considered crossed eyes and flat foreheads to be beautiful. To help their children become cross-eyed, mothers would tie boards to their children's heads and tie wax beads in front of their eyes to encourage them to look in that direction. Scars were considered marks of courage and attractiveness, and it was common for men and women to cut their skin to achieve the scarring design they wanted. The elites in the society would sharpen their teeth to a sharp point and make incrustations with jadeite or gold, a sign of beauty and wealth.

The dance was another ritual to Maya culture where lavish costumes would be prepared and ornaments such as staffs, rattles, live snakes, and spears would be used. The costumes would depict the forms of the divinities. By dressing and acting like a god, the Maya believed that the god's spirit would overtake them, and they would be able to communicate with the deity to ask for their prayers to be answered.

Maya folk medicine was based on a belief of health being a result of living peacefully in society and illness being a consequence of the gods for misbehavior. Medicine was only practiced by those who had received an extensive education. They were called *shamans* and were meant to act as a messenger between the physical and spiritual world. Another word archaeologists have found is *ah-men*, which means "disease throwers."

Archaeologists have found in Maya medical texts that herbal remedies were used according to the color of the original plant. They are as follows:

> Red: for rashes, blood disorders, burns
> Yellow: a disease of the liver and spleen (color of bile)
> Blue: natural sedatives
> White: avoided because it was seen as a signal of death

Common plants that are believed to have been used in medicine include but are not limited to chili peppers, cacao, agave, and tobacco. Animal parts from fish, insects, birds, and crocodiles could also be combined into an herbal recipe. Plants would also be rubbed onto the skin in the form of plaster to protect the body from bad spirits.

It is believed *shamans* would commonly use mind-altering substances such as "magic" mushrooms, peyote, tobacco, and other hallucinogens found in nature. These hallucinogens were believed to be a way of communicating with the gods to plead for health and to ask mercy for sins, in hopes that the gods would restore the balance in a person and bring back their health. If not able to provide a cure, these hallucinogens would at least be used to give pain relief. Self-brewed alcoholic concoctions would also be used. Maya pottery and carvings depict ritualistic enemas to ensure quick absorption of the substance.

Other common traditional cures involved prayer, offerings, and sweat baths. Similar to today's modern saunas, sweat bath chambers were made of stone walls and ceilings with an opening at the top for air to be expelled. The Maya believed the steam created in this environment was the perfect way for the body to expel impurities and restore the balance in a sick individual. Newly pregnant women would seek revitalization in a sauna, while the sick would hope to heal themselves. Even Maya rulers are believed to have frequently visited the sweat baths in their region because it left them feeling refreshed and able to think more clearly when making decisions for their people. In Piedras Negras, a city from the Classic Period whose structural remains are in Guatemala, archaeologists have discovered eight stone buildings that were used as sweat baths.

Maya medicine, like many other concepts of their society, was all about balance. For example, in medicine, it was a hot and cold balance. If someone had a "cold" disorder such as cramps or constipation, they would be treated with hot, spicy foods. If they had a "hot" disorder such as diarrhea, vomiting, or fever, they would be treated with cold plants or cold foods.

Evidence has also been found that the Maya *shamans* demonstrated surgical skills as well. They sutured open wounds with human hair and would reset bones. There have even been marks found that show they drilled into skulls with primitive drills. Dental surgeons would file teeth into shapes and insert decorative pieces made from gold, jade, turquoise, or other organic material. This was often done by the nobility as a sign of wealth and rank. Dental prostheses have also been found to assist those who may have lost teeth in battle.

Even today, male religious fraternities called *cofradias* have worked to preserve the steps and history of the traditional Maya dances. These men take their knowledge of the ancient dances as a very serious responsibility, researching and perfecting the dances and ensuring they will be passed to the next generation in the most authentic form they can. The Pop Wuj dance is done to show the four stages of creation that the Maya believe humans went through: the Man of Mud who did not praise the gods, the Man of Wood who was too rigid and was destroyed by the gods, the Monkey Man who was too silly and ultimately was also destroyed, and the Human Being, the current Maya, who prays to the gods to thank and praise them.

The Maya game Poc-a-Toc, which was technically a ballgame, had a much more religious significance than being just a pastime. Seven men would make up a team, and two teams would play on the ball court to gain points by scoring a rubber ball through a hoop on the far wall. Sometimes, the hoop would be as high as twenty feet, sometimes higher. They would also have to defend their own goal. The unique and impressive thing about it is that using hands and feet was against the rules: only their hips, head, knees, and shoulders were to be used. Diego de Landa, a Spanish bishop, wrote that watching the game being played was like watching "lightning" because the Maya players moved so quickly. Written records of how the game was played were destroyed by the Conquistadors, so researchers learned of it through oral history passed down the generations. It was previously believed that the team that lost would be killed at the completion of the match, but historians have analyzed glyphs and archaeological evidence to infer that even the winning team or captain could be killed to give them a quick path to heaven. Prisoners of war would be forced to play against the Maya in a reenactment of the war. The losers, the prisoners from a different city who could not play the game well, would be executed.

The game is symbolic of the Hero Twins' victory over the underworld lords, but it also hints at the Maya's cyclical belief of all things in nature. It is obvious from the human sacrifices that this was more than just an amusing game for Maya but a deep, spiritual part of their life and that the men who were chosen to play were honored by the society.

Chapter 12: Maya Technology

We have already spoken at length of how advanced the Maya numeral system was, as well as their knowledge of the number zero and how this led to their very accurate calculations regarding the astronomical lunar and solar cycle. Alongside this, it is also important to note the other advancements of this civilization.

For example, the elaborate temples and great cities that are still present to this day were all built without the essential modern tools of metal or the wheel. Other Mesoamerican civilizations used the wheel and found it extremely helpful, but the Maya did not use it because they did not domesticate animals like those other societies. Without animals to carry the cart, the Maya developed a different device called the tumpline, or *mecapal*. It allowed them to carry 125 pounds on their back comfortably. There was a strap connected to a frame to support heavy loads.

The Maya built their huge structures out of limestone, carefully crafted and built to withstand the worst of the weathering over centuries. The Maya arch, as it has become known, was a method they independently employed, achieving the look of the Classic Western arch. They did so without shaping the stone structures, however, as they could not do so without the proper tools. Despite the foundational problems of the arch, it is still an achievement for the Maya and a distinct feature in their style of architecture.

They did use some innovations in their arts such as looms for weaving cloth and creating an array of colorful, metallic paints from mica, a mineral that still has its use in technology and making pigment paints today. They were also adept at making tools out of jadeite stone. The Maya did not have access to iron ore—the only ore source in Mexico is over a thousand miles north of the ancient Maya Empire. Because of this, the Maya dedicated black jadeite for use in their tools. On a scale of 1 to 10 of mineral hardness (the maximum is 10 for a diamond), jadeite falls between a 6.5 and 7. It is harder than even steel or iron. It is believed these were the principal tools used by sculptors, wood carvers, and artisans alike, as archaeologists have found jadeite tools in various shapes such as chisels, axes, hoes to indicate their employment in multiple ways and professions. Green jadeite is most popular in jewelry, but black jadeite, when the aluminum in the compound is replaced by iron to produce an isomorph compound, shows great strength due to the prismatic crystals in the chemical makeup. It is believed now that the Maya sourced black jadeite from the tectonic plate in the Montagua Valley of Guatemala.

The interesting thing is that archaeologists did not find these tools in the royal tombs of the dead kings. It can be inferred from this that these tools were passed down from artisan families and were kept in the lineage because of how valuable they were for their crafts. The skills, along with the tools, would be passed down to a new generation of learners. Obsidian, a volcanic glass found in a ring of volcanoes along the Pacific coast, was also used for making even stronger blades for knives and swords meant for use in battle.

The Maya was also the first civilization in Mesoamerica to build the equivalent of modern roads. Called *sacbe*, these roads were built along their jungle environment to facilitate travel between their city-states. This would have been very necessary because trading with their neighboring states was very important to the local economy. The roads were paved, and the trees and leaves around them were cut to make it more comfortable for travelers. Traveling kings used these roads, as well as traders who traveled the city-states for commerce.

Another important innovation to note is that of rubber. It is commonly believed that the vulcanization of rubber with other materials came from Charles Goodyear in America in the 19th century. But now historians are giving the Maya credit for producing rubber products three thousand years before Goodyear even came up with the concept in the late 1800s. Researchers believe that the Maya may have stumbled upon this process accidentally, such as through a religious ritual where they may have used the rubber tree. Once they realized how strong the plant was, they used it in a variety of ways such as making water-resistant clothes, binding for their books and tablets, and making large rubber balls that were used in their traditional game of Poc-a-Toc.

Chapter 13: Maya People Today

Today, there are descendants of the Maya people who occupy southern Mexico, northern Honduras, Guatemala, and Belize. They are a people fiercely protective of their heritage. They speak their native languages, wear traditional clothing, and practice their ancient religion. The term "Maya" is a broad term referring collectively to the descendants of the people of that region, but after centuries of migration, there are many distinct societies and populations of Maya people with their own cultures and traditions that mirror the equally distinct societies of their ancestors. The belief that the Maya simply vanished because their cities were found abandoned is untrue. There are nearly six million Maya today who perform and adhere to their ancient traditions, and they would find the idea that their culture has vanished as insulting.

Guatemala, southern Mexico, Belize, El Salvador, the Yucatán Peninsula, and western Honduras have numerous populations that adhere to the ancient Maya culture. These cultures are also immersed in Hispanicized Mestizo culture due to the Spanish colonization, but some sects continue to emulate a traditional way of life, even speaking the Mayan language as a primary language. Anthropologists identify the most prevalent Maya language today as "Yucatec Maya," but speakers refer to it as simply "Maya." Spanish is most commonly a second or first language due to the prevalence of Spanish culture in the region. Today, the Academia de Lenguas Mayas (the Guatemalan Academy of Maya Languages) exists and works to preserve the language of the Maya in Guatemala in a world where ancient languages are on the verge of being lost.

Though the region was influenced strongly by Christianity due to the 16th century conquest and the spread of colonialism, there are still old ways that are observed with a mix of Catholicism and Mayan mysticism. On Cozumel Island, shrines to the ancient goddess Ix Chel and the Virgin Mary are both present, and they are seen as one divinity. The Daykeeper of a village still has the Maya role of interpreting the energy of a day. Mayan rituals are performed in caves and on the same terrain where their ancestors once practiced.

The most famous Maya on the global stage is Quiche Indian Rigoberta Menchu, the recipient of the 1992 Nobel Peace Prize for her work in social justice fighting for the rights of indigenous people. She is a well-known activist, fighting for the rights of the Maya people to practice their culture and region, as well as for feminist rights. Though there were some controversies that arose later regarding her recollections for her autobiography, the Nobel Committee dismissed calls to revoke her Nobel Peace Prize. She is also a UNESCO Goodwill Ambassador and has run for President of Guatemala in 2007 and 2011. Despite losing in the first round both times, in 2007, she gave a heartfelt message of peace on television for all Guatemalans.

Conclusion

Thank you for making it through to the end of *Maya Civilization*. Let's hope it was informative and able to provide you with a background of the ancient Maya civilization and the history of its people. We wanted to include information on the timeline of the Maya so that the growth of their civilization can be charted. They went from being a collection of small groups to being builders of huge temples and pyramids, growing nearly a dozen different types of plants to provide for their population. At one time, the biggest Maya cities could have been home to nearly 100,000 people. Considering these structures were built without modern tools or even the assistance of the wheel to carry stones, this was an impressive feat for the Maya, showcasing the intellectual capacity of the civilization.

Information on their cultural traditions had also been covered, as well as their religion, architecture, and their advanced knowledge in the fields of mathematics and astronomy. Despite being a Stone Age society, their calculations on the lunar and solar calendar were very close to today's calculations. Among many other things, we also learned about the Maya calendar and how they grouped together years to form a unique concept of time.

The next step is to dive deeper into Maya artifacts, visit their museums or ancient temples, and view their stone carvings that exist to this day. A trip to Central America to truly appreciate their ancient sites might be required, but it will surely be worth it. There are many museums open in the region that honor the Maya history, and descendants today can even perform traditional dances and sell their hand-crafted goods.

Finally, if you found this book useful in any way, a review on Amazon is always appreciated!

www.ingramcontent.com/pod-product-compliance
Lightning Source LLC
Chambersburg PA
CBHW052208110526
44591CB00012B/2132